Dedicated to Marie

For making me feel loved for who I am

Eric Rosenqvist

101 poems for highly sensitive persons

Struggle and Acceptance

Impressum

© 2023 Eric Rosenqvist

Framsida: Eric Rosenqvist

Förlag: BoD – Books on Demand, Stockholm, Sverige
Tryck: BoD – Books on Demand, Norderstedt, Tyskland

ISBN: 978-91-8057-443-3

FOREWORD

A few years ago, I came into contact with the concept high sensitivity and HSP (high sensitive person). I read books, websites, stories from other highly sensitive persons and did tests. It was very clear to me that I was highly sensitive. It didn't change my reality, but it gave me explanations for why I always felt different, why I didn't seem to be able to function like others. I'm not going to explain what HSP is or how it works, there are already a number of very good books for that and some I would like to mention are "The Highly Sensitive Person", by Elaine N. Aron and "The Highly Sensitive Man" by Tom Falkenstein.

I have come to terms with the fact that I am a seeker and I now understand that it is part of the highly sensitive personality trait. With this knowledge I want to reach out to other highly sensitive persons who are also searching for their place, their context, their well-being and their life. I've always written. It's a way of being for me. Now I write more than ever. When I've looked back at the poems I've written over the years, I see that many of them are about searching, about not fitting

7

in, about being different, but also about having an enormously strong drive to create, to be creative, and that it can be a way to exist.

Many of the poems are dark, some really dark, but I believe that there are other highly sensitive persons who have felt and thought similarly. Maybe my poems can be helpful by showing that you are not alone in this. That the darkness can exist with acceptance instead of being fought and that it is possible to find light even where and when it is darkest. We cannot ignore the darkness; we cannot pretend that it does not exist. It exists. It is part of us and therefore has the right to exist. Expressing the darkness through writing and reading or other creativity can be a way to get it out and thus give it an opportunity to sink away and release its grip on you. You may even be able to direct that energy into something constructive instead of destructive.

Most of the poems were written before I knew the concept of high sensitivity. The poems can convey that this is our reality and it's ok. It may still be hard and difficult but you are not wrong as a human being. You are ok as a human being and this is part of what we go through as highly sensitive persons.

1

There seem to be no openings
Out
Despite the inflow
No outflow
Despite incoming
No outgoing
Levels are being raised
Increasing pressure
For those of us who are there
Who want to escape
Who want to create something
Something that can get out
Something that can grow and flourish
But it continues to rise
With us in
But we keep looking
After an opening, a crack, a joint
It is the only thing we can do

Until we disappear

2

Cut thin strips

to see

the blood

the creation that is being destroyed

because it feels right

to do wrong

the words that hurt more than the blows

the fear that confuses itself

because there are threats from all sides

from outside

from inside

there is no me after

just an abnormal mass

one it

of fear

the destructive

taking its place

at the expense

of

the constructive

the creative

3
Titles
That weighs
Costumes
Which are ill-fitting
Proper footwear
Which chafe
Templates
Where I don't fit
The context
Where I don't belong
Forms
Which should be malleable yet it is I who am being shaped
The time
when to be awake
The time
when to be a sleep
Issues
To be resolved
Because it can't go on like this
There must be an improvement
Methods for everything
As long as you want it, it's possible
They say
I am bleeding from fatigue
Wounds should be washed, stitched up
The scar should be taped so as not to be ugly
But I keep bleeding
Living, breathing, bleeding
What cannot be fixed remains

4

I care too much

Can't help it

It is just so

Therefore

Distances

Periodic insulation

A lifesaver pushed under the surface by the person in distress

Words that never stop echoing

Wounds that keep opening up

Time to heal in privacy

5

Contouring the colors
Provides depth
The clouds are retreating
What remains is the clear blue
Under the grass
Clay
Heavy, dense, compact
The moisture changes its color
The hole has
A certain depth
A certain dimension
Where the color stays

6

Feeling the dirt under foot soles
Embodies the eternal
Order and chaos
It is not possible to make the dirt disappear
The disintegration

Does not take me further
Everything feels fragile
Crumbles between fingers

7

From all sides
By all means
Are they trying to push me into the mold
This is the way to be
I do not fit
Have never done
Will never do
But you should
For all others, it fits
They bring out tools, instruments
Bands, carves, attracts, threatens
And
Presses
I break into pieces
As I have done every time before
Tearing open old wounds
New wounds are added
Because the tools are hard
Has sharp edges
The mold does not give in
Non-formable
If we just take away this and this
So it will fit
You will see
Those parts are of no use to you anyway.
Right?
It's just wrong
We will fix that
If you just do and be like everyone else, it will work out.
Don't worry, we will help you
Becoming
As we

Otherwise, you can go to hell. If you can't perform, you have no business being here.

8

There is the fatigue
Which I can't do anything about
Which I can't help
But I don't have the energy
Wants to be alert
Want to be proud and beautiful
Can't cope

9

Black ice

I'm slipping, sliding

The foothold is lost

Hear how joints twist and break when I fall

The black and cold meets me

Crushes me

Blood in the mouth, in the eyes

Climbing up and forward

Only to fall

Again

And get smashed

Again

There is nothing in either direction

Above me

The night

Below me

Black ice

10

The chains are forged from the purest and strongest material

Meticulous and insane craftsmanship

The iron ring around the neck

Stifling every thought of screaming

Veins swell like snakes

Up to the faceless skull

Of rage

Anger my name

Fear is yours

Reinforced concrete around me, under me

Ten meters up, an iron grid

Letting the beast see the black sky and storm clouds

Does the anger disappear

No

Reducing anger

No

11

So, I stand before you again. A new stage, a new place, a different time, but everything is the same. I give you the finger. For a moment you recoil. You were prepared for me to smile and tell you that everything is fine and that there are no problems. That everything is under control and that I will solve it for you. I tell you to fuck off and leave me alone. Leave me alone. Let me live my life.

Without your permission.

The spotlight doesn't leave me for a second. It's hot, sweat is breaking out and you're still there. I'm trapped in that damn light, on that damn stage in front of your eyes. I want to go out. Leave everything behind. Through the back door to the back streets. Pull up your hood and roam along flaking facades. Walk into the dirtiest bar, order the strongest drink. Pour it down my throat as a statement. This is where it ends. This is where it begins. Pick up the phone, call my wife and say "it's over now, it's actually over, I'm free".

But I remain standing on the stage. Unable to leave. Your eyes won't let me go. They demand, demand and demand. Someone shouts from the darkness of the salon " Why should you get off the hook? Who do you think you are?"

Is he right? Why should I get away with it?

12

Now is the time
Let strength dispel your doubts
Do what needs to be done
Meet your enemy
Your fears
Stand up, show yourself
It all depends on you

13
Shielded
Forgetting how he did it
The words no longer taste good
The tongue curls up
Rest is a better choice
Hands are stretched out
Poking at him
Contemptuously rejects them
Attracting them
Drowning them

14

Has burned everything
Starting over
An attempt to free myself from all the demands, habitual patterns
What I should do
Is expected to do
It is not easy
Maybe there is something good there
Maybe there is a part of me there
But now it is too late
Everything is burnt
Over
No room for reflection
No time for regrets

15

They walk around in all their glory
Are involved
Important
Important to someone
I am not part of anything
Have been invited to participate
Took the wrong door and went out again
Indifference
Nothing
Except
Indifference

16
Feet are knocked away
Falls
Does not reach the ground
Being in the falling
In the midst of a stumbling movement
No control
No routines or habitual patterns
Just the falling
Only that

17

I know it is there
The Darkness
It has always been there
Occasional reminders
Demonstrated by cracks in the facade
It is clear that it is there
Why shouldn't be there?
There is a monster, a beast, in that darkness
A force of nature without laws
Inside some of us
Inside me

18

I question myself

And why shouldn't I

What am I doing here

What am I supposed to do

Why should I take my dreams seriously when no one else
does?

Just press the button

Anguish

Doubt

Letting the doubts come

Stay with me

And then I let it fade away

At its own pace

Because I know that I am with myself

Because I know that darkness is not truer than light just
because it's dark

19

You wanted solitude, right?
Here it is in all its glory
Isn't it beautiful?
You don't have to adapt to someone else
No consideration
You don't have to explain why you are the way you are
Why you're not like others
You can sit there completely isolated
And all the time you have left over
All the books, films, series, songs you can enjoy
How many invented lives you can follow instead of your own?
It might be a bit lonely sometimes
A little passive
A bit self-pitying
But it's for the best, right?
For now
You no longer have to feel like
a disappointment
a burden
You no longer need to feel that
you are hurting them
you are letting them down
you have to perform in order to exist
You can just sit there
That's what you wanted, right?

20

Trying to move upwards
Want to get up and out
Wet and heavy soil collapses
There is no air here
There is no room
No space
For anything at all
That is me

21
It shifts
A switch beyond my control
Burning
Sizzling in my veins
Wanting only the dark

22

I need walls
Fortifications
Against what tries to get in
Eventually makes its way in
Not leaving my mind alone
Takes on an attitude of protection
Which gives me some leeway
Distancing yourself from what's going on
The hard exterior
My armor

23

Lead me

Show me the direction

Show me the way

Someone to trail

Simplify what I can't understand

Let everything slow down

A water mirror

No ripples

No movements

No shadows

Just blank emptiness

24
Condemned without hope
Untamed primal force
Wants to turn the world upside down
Shout out everything that is wrong
Facing violence with superiority
Intimidate
Then purify

25

They extend their hands
Wants to grab me
I have led them
Attracting them to me
Because I could do it
Yesterday
I had the energy
Yesterday
To be a part of the community
Today I am retreating
Trying to dismiss the hands being stretched out
Because I can't face them
Today
I don't have the energy
Today

26

Cause after cause
Take me to the place
To the point
To the state
Where fear prevails
Concern about not functioning
In the sense of meeting the requirements
In the sense of being normal
In the sense of being like others
The brain is spinning with this concern
Activating me
Refuses me rest

27

- I'm sure you're absolutely right, I say. I'm probably not really healthy. And it's probably so simple that if I just get well, everything will be fine again. Then I won't have to wonder what's wrong with me. Why I'm not like them.

- You are absolutely right, I continue, that I have caused this myself. That I only have myself to blame. And if I just try, it will get better. That all I have to do is make up my mind and try really hard and things will get better.

28
The only thing that exists then is the work
The process of writing one word after another
And then another
The only thing that can focus the mind
The discipline to stick to what is mine
The discipline to make my own life interesting
Not to be distracted by all the chatter going around
Temptations that attract
I adapt too well
Until my profile and character is filed down
Flattening
Time for fellowship
Time for solitude
Just fix my gaze on
My doing

29

You are in me
Living in me
My fear
You want to tell me something
Tell me what I need to know
That I should be on my guard
Aware of real danger
Ready to run away, escape, hide
I thank you for what you do
Saving me
But I want to tell you something too
That my desire to do, just the doing
That it should also be allowed to exist
A space to do and be without fear
To dare

30

It feels good to talk to you
Let the pen caress the paper
Here I am
My whole self
Nothing left out
Fear is an emotion
Emotions are matter
Writing is the expression of emotions
Take your emotions out of your body and look at them from
a distance
Pacify you
Trust me when I tell you everything is fine

31
So much to give
Love that gives birth to love
Everything I want to do
And give you

32

Longing in the chest
The driving force
Is in me
Alongside the turmoil
And the restlessness
Want to create
Want to reach out
Want to help
Touching the knowledge
About what I can give the world

33

So much I want to do
So much I want to say
Stories that want to be told
Making different voices heard
Through all these words
All these sentences
Through the noise we live in
To people who cover their ears and shut themselves in
For people who turn up the volume even more
Always higher
Always more
Stories bouncing off walls in stairwells
In through letterboxes
Landing on the hallway carpet
To you
For you
An attempt to reach you
Being there for you
With stories

34
All the time closer
Than before
Constantly driven
Constantly the desire
To create new

35

In the movement
There is tranquil
And its opposite
In the stillness
There is tranquil
And its opposite
Present
Monitoring
Motivational

36

First nothing
And then
Now
So much that everything moves
Vibrations that propagate
Spreading through us
And further
Always further

37
What is true for me
Do I decide
It's not in your hands
This is me
Here I am

38
Time disappears
Ceases
A constant flow
An interior in constant motion
An exterior that you think you recognize
Tells you very little about what is going on
Where thoughts are already conceived
Where fear protects and inhibits
But always
A constant flow

39

Words find their way onto paper
Unaccustomed to being shaped
Resisting the movement
And give in

Nurture the qualities that are you
Where you are in a state of being and doing
Not because you should
Not for anyone else
Than yourself

40

I just want to tell you over and over again
How much I love you
How beautiful I am when you see me
The real me

Candles are lit in the windows
Raises hope
Always light
Always hope

41

Being in the flow
Is the most intense
Nothing stronger
Or more clearly
Sharp contours to cling on to
Helps me stay put
In the flow
Releases
Thorns against
And continues

42

A place
My place
Where is it located?
Does not fit in
Fits all too well
Adapting myself
Chameleon
Letting myself get lost in role after role
The roles they want me to play
The outside world
It is the roles I take on
That they like
When I, my self, shine through, they fear
Taking a step backwards
Too strange
Too different
They do not know how to behave
Is he normal today or not?
They want me to put on the mask
Acting the roles
But only just enough
Not too much

43

Misplaced
Confused
Lost
Was I supposed to do something?
Was I destined for something?
When did it go by?
Did I notice it?
There is a template to follow
A mold to be cast in
A framework to stay within
I don't fit there
Not really
Is there any place outside?
Outside of all that was intended
A place for me

44
Start with what is true
What you believe in
But if I don't know
If the truth is to lie
If believing is not believing
How should I then
Start
How should I then
Continue
How should I then
Take me further
How should I then
Stop

45

It flickers
White lines
Dark background
Tingling sensations in what has been numb
Movement in what has been still
Turmoil in what has been calm
What space is it possible to give yourself?

There is a new day ahead of me
Not feeling the excitement and anticipation I want to feel
Want to do something
Just get started and see where it goes
Without plans or goals

46

Dwelling on the doubt

I have learned that what I feel is

Self-pity

Nothing else

But just that

How do I go against what I believe in

What I believe to be true

What I hold closest

Why are the forces against each other

How can this division exist in an interconnected thing?

How can two wills emerging from the same nucleus coexist?

How can I be in it

47

I choose not to participate
Standing on the sidelines
Just watch as you continue
And continues
I can't be there
Only too well
There is almost nothing left now
And then what?
When you have continued all the way through
And I am still standing
Wondering what happened
What I missed
If I would have followed
If I would have come along
Stepped on
Joined you
See it so clearly
All escape routes
All readiness and preparation
If I am unable to participate
Withdrawal

48

The edges are sharp, stained with rust. A network of fine scars on the fingertips. Attempt after attempt to grasp the edge, to get underneath with your fingers and lift. Clear the way.

49

I am on my way

I am moving

Sometimes I feel like I've forgotten the way, but I'm moving.

In the strange darkness

In the illuminated streets

Ultimately, nothing is important that does not concern me

Give in to the feeling of discomfort that I haven't done what

I should have done today

Making the most of what I think is me

Without anyone looking over my shoulder

Without any censorship whatsoever

Alone

Just for now

Just for what I need to do

To be true

To be me

50

There is no longing there
Just reality
It is getting up every morning
Take the bus to work
Sitting in the office
Writing reports to make money for the owners
Some are pissed off just because I'm sitting there
Some are happy for me to see them
Then there is no more
A livelihood
A profession
No space
For dreams
For desires

51

I have left it behind

Landed outside Reykjavik this morning

Sitting on a bench now and letting the Icelandic wind blow
through me

Letting it live through me

I'm so cold that I'm shaking but I don't know anything else

Only here

Only now

The decision is mine regardless of the consequences

Control or not

I am here

Now

52

I can't stand the superficiality
I can't stand the falsehood
I close the doors behind me
locks them
but there is no energy
no power
just being there
in their midst
among us

53
The razor blades cut through the corneas
Leaves scars in the field of vision

I am hiding even though I know better

54

They took his pride
torched it
Buried it in decaying spasms
Asked him to leave his home

He cursed their tongues
Their insightfulness

Corrected itself and removed everything that shouldn't be

Only what is expected
Only what exists

I asked them to listen
They cursed me
I listened to them
They cursed me
I appealed in the face of what I believed to be true
They cursed me
I corrected myself
They forgot about me

55

They hid those who could not cope and said they did not exist

That all that you saw was also all there was

Making mistakes
Is to fail
Not succeeding
Is to fail
Failure
Is to fail

We erase all weaknesses
These are the requirements we set for you and ask you to choose.
All other routes are a failure
Until you prove otherwise
Then we'll celebrate you as one of the few
You shall let the wounds on your knuckles heal, the scars fade away.
Pretend to be preoccupied with the important things that made you who you are and throw words of wisdom at anyone who tries to prove it.
That
It's not freedom if you don't take it

56

I travel in the light of dawn

Bought myself a worn-out car. Needed to do something, needed to move. It felt like a compulsion. A compulsion that I had to make the decisions myself.

That the choices are mine.

That my life is mine.

Even something as simple as traveling at dawn in a car where the heating doesn't work and your fingers are stiff around the steering wheel.

Being on the road.

Is my decision.

Being on the road.

57

In the glow of darkness, we cover our wounded bodies
It is something that is there
Something we cannot see or touch
But we know
A sensation we have repressed
Forgotten what it is
Only that it is
When they get through, we can't handle it
We are intimidated

Backing away
All blood disappears
Pale faces
The shadow of perception hides it again

The color comes back
We stand there and pretend
That we were never intimidated
That it was not so bad
That it's nothing to worry about

But we know

Our shadows are visible
In the glow of darkness

58
Keeping me constantly on the move
Not allowing wounds to heal
Blood clotting
Text on paper
Yet so much
Need to express something
Restlessness is put to rest
The mind calms down
The paper is filled with text

59

A man is sitting there writing. He wants to tell something. He wants to tell it in a way that gives people something. He wants to tell stories to fill his days with meaning. He walks across the winter-dirty streets, between the houses where millions of people live and wonders what he is really doing. He wants to reduce complexity to the core of inherent meaning.

"I long", he writes, but he can't get any further. Because if he longs, it means he wants to be somewhere else and that feels like a betrayal. He erases the words and writes:

"I am and I long". That's how it is. Through the forests and across the fields. A journey without end, without destination, where he always is because there is no end and always longs because there is no beginning.

He has written his line and saves it.

60
I am a stranger here
In the middle of life
In the middle of lunch

Sitting alone with my coffee, my pen and my notebook
Try to gather your impressions
An attempt to understand what is happening around me

Does the pressure never ease? asks the man at the bottom of
the rubbish pile that we build daily with the waste products
of our achievements
Does the pressure never ease?

It is easy to become speed blind
And not notice
I try hard not to see
To drown out all impressions
Seems to demand its place

A myriad of unwilling actions
Decisions taken to make things as good as possible and
drive us forward in development
The wheels should turn
People should run
We know nothing else

61

In the midst of that
A chaos of which I am a part
A massive pressure to perform
There is no time to stop and think.
There is a next that is never now

Now will very soon be then and therefore we opt out now
and reach for the next one
New information, new contacts
At the same time
The wheels are turning, they said.

I get tired
Feeling that the contours are blurred in a haze
A torrent that washes over me and sometimes it doesn't
even seem worth trying to reach for that branch that sticks
out.
The branch that can, if only for a moment, give me a fixed
point to cling to and stop.
If I turn my head, I see the beach going by

Going against the current without feeling the bottom under
your feet is doomed to failure.

62

What did you think would happen?

Accusing myself

Blaming

Darkness

Hate

Holocaust

Not daring to be myself

Don't dare

The perfect betrayal

Total defeat

Don't know how to get out

Digging downwards instead of climbing upwards

Moist heavy soil instead of the sun

The frustration

Rage

Contempt

Who am I?

Where am I going?

Is there something about myself that I want?

Yes

A beginning that can hopefully become an end

A healthy ending

A clean cut without infection

Just scar to remember where I have been

63

I pick up old notes. They are both a symbol and an archive of who I have been and who I have become.

I find that I am outside the community if I choose to do so. And why should I have a choice?

The city is full of people and they are all on the move. Belonging consists of being part of this crowd. Exclusion is choosing a different path.

I recognize myself from my old words. When I read them, I feel as if I have let myself down, yet I am now closer than ever.

64

Dull, lifeless
A bad taste in the mouth and a tiring headache
Still, on the road
Soothing movement
Gives me a task
To travel
And finally
Finding home

65

Autumn sets in
Wistfulness cannot be pushed aside anymore
I dream of a kind of excellence
But not here
Time wanders and takes us through the rain and colors of
autumn
I have a feeling in my chest that there is something I ought
to do
Listening to myself and filling the gaps
Picking up the thread and trying to find the meaning again

Presence with those I love

Give hope to those who try

Peace for me and the feeling in my chest

66
When pride digs the grave
What is left?
More death
Misery
A wounded body
A shattered life

Someone is putting their faith and trust at risk
And slowly there is an awakening

Something barer and purer is taking shape
The tattoos pale in comparison to the experience gained

Everything fades, is obscured in this new shadow

67

I am moving
For real this time
On the road, mile after mile
I leave behind me

When darkness falls
If I fall through

There is something enticing and tragic about the lonely journey
It is a journey without a destination and without a home to come back to
Is it even a journey?
Rather an escape or a condition

But it is not me
Never been

68

A chilly wind finds its way between clothes
The sound of water
The colors are pale, dull, pleasant
Exhalation
Trying to understand
Insight
There was something that was forgotten
At the far end
Making attempts futile

69
Trying to get rid of
The indifference
The relentless stubbornness that keeps asking why?
What is the point of that?
At the same time
Don't want to get rid of it
There is no better protection
No better place to hide
Nowhere else to hide

70

It does not lead to progress
No genuine motivation
Living in denial
Living a lie is lying to someone else
Living a true lie is lying to yourself without knowing it
Living an untrue lie is lying to yourself and knowing it, an active choice
There is no honesty there
No purity
But there is a sense of security
Something to always fall back on
My untrue lie
I justify
My untrue lie

71

There is something inside
That wants to get out
Needs an intermediary
Someone to make its voice heard
The words that get out
The stories that get out
Are shadowless

72

Trying to make my voice heard
Over the roar
Over a thousand voices murmuring
Feeling my way
Can't get through
The itch
All over the body
Angry scratching
Want to find the cooling wind
The carrying wave
Where I can work
And
Get done

73

Longing
Somewhere in there
Settling down
Looking towards that horizon
Know that feeling
Still waiting
Biding its time
It is the sensible thing to do
The logical thing to do
That's what I learned
At the same time, where is the sense and logic in not doing
what you want?
That voice I hear
Not listening
There is always something else
Than
Longing

74

Yes, I know
I hide the sides that are not accepted
I play a role
It makes everything much better
Because then it doesn't show
We pretend that the dark sides don't exist

That there are parts of me, my person, that we hide
We don't have to think about that

75
Breaking point
Time to choose
Realize that it is ultimately up to me
Need to be true
True to myself
Don't need those performances anymore
They are not true
Because ultimately it depends on me
Always
Me

76

Have tried to choose that joy

But

I look for and provoke reasons and causes to spew out negativity?

Indifference

Nothing appeals

Everything can be questioned and criticized

Passivity

If I say nothing, I cannot say wrong

If I do nothing, I cannot do wrong

But at the same time

The indifference is not the fear of doing wrong

It is about indifference

It is about questioning the point and the fun of something you usually do or would like to do.

It is about passivity

A thousand and one things are waiting to be done or at least could be done

Why? asks indifference

Wants to be some kind of victim

Wants to provoke incomprehension in others

Through passivity

Wouldn't have time anyway

No, don't feel like it

Attracting advice

Just to dismiss them

Attracting helping hands

Just to cut them off

Just to show what a victim I am

Why

To criticize and dismiss ideas
To provoke incomprehension
Is to hurt others
Enough times and the damage is done
Must not forget to question indifference
Behind it I cannot help others
Only hurt them

Often, if not always, something triggers it. Then I hold it
and wallow in it.
Better to lock yourself up then
Beating cold concrete walls
Stare at the silent phone
And finally write it down
It is then easier to return to the usual truths
But it must be done

Know or begin to understand that I am the one who chooses
and is responsible for my choices.
Indifference calls it into question
There is a salvation in doing
In the action itself
When indifference questions everything
Push through
By doing

As I said, I have tried to choose joy
This is the attempt

77

Help us

They say

Because they know I want to help

They know they can come to me even if I am occupied

I will listen

On their problems

What they feel

That I will help them move forward

I can't help it

Can't pretend not to hear

Can't pretend not to feel

It echoes in me later

Continues to feel

After they have moved on

Can't help you and you at the same time

Can't help you and you and me at the same time

Hence the distance

To you

Who wants my help

Otherwise

Nothing left

78

End up there by my own power

Closing myself in

It's something I know

Learned in silence

Know that it is not a good place

Not if you want to be a whole person

On the other hand

Not many people are whole

It is a better place than many others

It is possible to breathe there when it is not possible to breathe anywhere else

It is possible to create there or rather create to get out of there

It is possible to destroy there

Everything can be destroyed from there

Annihilate myself and everything connected to my person

A violent force that cannot be stopped or mitigated

Always available

Never more than a word or a gesture away

Never

Never

The roars do not stop

They increase

79
So
The shame
Not being able to handle
What others can handle
What others do
How others socialize
How others work
How others celebrate

In the comparison
There is only the destructive

80
Under the knife
The sharp scalpel
Cutting off what is me
Shaping the self
To appease
Appease the masses
The cuts are neat
The scars become just white lines

There was a boy sitting there playing his guitar. What do you want to do when you grow up? They asked him.

- Play the guitar. It's fun.
- Shouldn't you have a real job? It's good to have, they said.

There was a teenage boy standing outside the music store looking at a shiny electric guitar.

- It's great that you have a hobby, something to do in your spare time, but what are you going to do after high school? Are you going to study further?

There was a young man sleeping well into the morning after a late gig the night before.

- It's time for him to get on with his life now. Get a job. He can't sleep all day, they said behind his back. It's time to stop dreaming and start living.

A middle-aged man sings and plays on a huge stage in front of thousands and thousands of people.

- How brilliant he is. There has always been something special about him. So gifted and born with such talent.

82

I sense somewhere that there are things that I should do now
Before it is too late
Like showing who I am for example
For a brief moment
No, more
I got more
For several minutes I felt the warmth, the love
Understood by the feeling in the chest
Who I was
What I should do
I have a destination
To not hide myself

83

Trying to forgive
That bitterness has taken over... again
Concerns about the lack of confirmation are realized
You might think that you should have learned by now and
thus avoided the pain
But it is not possible
What would it look like
No it is not appropriate
Certainly not

84

Thoughts without attachments

Without beginning

Without end

With no destination, my struggle continues

Is there anything else?

That can feed my restlessness?

Seeking security

and peace

By the side of a safe harbor, the anchor is loosened to bring me out

At least I let my mind believe

That beyond the horizon

That's where I'll look to find my longing

That's where I will find answers

But for now

I'm still standing

85

Of course, it is an escape
It is not possible to say what the escape means
But to deny it is to deny oneself
Looking for a place, an occasion, a time, a feeling
Looking for an escape
Into the unknown
In order to hide
In order to show itself

86

Before it is too late

What or who decides when it is too late?

I travel through January darkness that holds a certain amount of light.

I tell myself that I have to show who I am before it is too late.

Days pass and sometimes it can feel like the noose is tightening.

The question is: what can I give?

Being absolutely present for people I hold close.

To deeply care for them and love them.

I do not always recognize the demands, needs and expectations that we are expected to live in.

I keep coming back to "There is something more".

Something that evokes that warm feeling in the chest.

It is easy to get lost and never see certain dimensions of life.

87

Where the road begins. That's where he longed to go.

He wanted to sit down and write down his thoughts, dreams and ideas. He wanted to put what he knew on paper and see people's reactions when they read what he wrote.

We know we are dying, he used to think. What should we do with that knowledge? Is it possible to use it as a fixed point to build life around? If time did not exist, would nothing move?

The car starts. He flicks a gear and releases the clutch. It wants to go forward. The car wants to go forward. The window is down and he hears the gravel crunching under the tires. It's early and by the time it's light he will have traveled a long way on the roads. The radio talk show's morning program will be coming to an end and he will probably want to stop and have a coffee somewhere.

He does not know where he wants to go or where he wants to get to. He knows that he wants to be on the road. To be in motion. He knows he wants to build his world but first he wants to understand the point of it.

88

A slight drunkenness or tiredness has got the better of me. I have difficulty thinking in a structured way. Things happen without my control and I don't get where I want to go, where I intend to go.

Need time, opportunity and routines to create. To be creative. Feels like a pointless repetition. Not getting around to doing what I feel I should be doing.
I'm going to write down my thoughts
Writing myself clean
Writing dirty
Writing repulsively
Writing cleanly
I will write my thoughts and collect them into a library of myself.
All ideas should be pinned
All ideas should be transcribed

89

We scattered our lives in a mosaic across the floor
To see if we fit
Was there any piece that was larger
That was me

A thin layer
A distance
Between me and the world
Cut off
Not quite there
Among you
One step away

90

Somewhere it had become too much
Or too little
Depending on how you looked at it
Too much of what he wanted to get away from
Too little of what he longed for
Always in search
To find a way forward
That the new path would lead to something more
To be a seeker

91

Noise
Propagating in the pipes
Through the walls
You don't want to hear them
Want to be left alone
Just be on your own
It's your safety
It's your comfort
Noise is getting closer and closer
Wants to get in
Waking you up
Take possession
You turn away
Putting your hands over your ears
Trying to shield yourself
Building the wall around you
Your refuge
The voices are coming soon
You know that
They did it yesterday
They are only silent for a moment
Then they start again
Just a brief moment of silence
After the noise
Before the voices
That's the worst of all
The nausea before the vomiting
No escape
Just being
In the present
Only that
And you

The voices speak to you
Overwhelms you
Hiding you in the noise
You don't want to
But can't
They take you
And you stay put
Safety grows and shrinks with your breathing.
Like the door beating in the wind
Never locked
Never open
Always noise
Voices from outside
Trying to influence your choice
But it is your choice
Always yours

92

Trying to write down
The wistfulness
Get it out of me
At the same time, I want to keep it
It is genuine
I know that
Something that cannot be ignored
Or touched

93

In this
I shall live
My life, my reality
There is no way to fight reality
I am dropping that fight
Replacing it with acceptance
Friendly voice
Gentle eyes
I don't need to fix myself
Just being with myself
This does not mean that I feel ok
It may still be just as difficult, just as hard
The suffering
But it means that I am ok as a human being
that I am not a mistake
that I am who I am supposed to be

I stand up
To face my reality

94
Five different decades
40 years
I have actually made it this far
Come all the way to this point
A bit surprised but still here
So for those who are struggling
Struggling to fix yourself
Struggling to correct the deficiencies so that you can be worthy
What if you are already ok
Just as you are right now
Just as you feel right now
What if you could instead be with yourself without that struggle?
Just be
If you can let go of that struggle and replace it with acceptance of who you are, relief and liberation follow.
The acceptance does not happen at one time
It must be continuous
Now your reality is like this
Can you be ok with that?
You are allowed to be you

95

On the way
After all
I see you
You are with me
After all
You have gone through
Are you still here
Full of life and passion
Full of anxiety
Because it could not be otherwise
I am here with you
I will always do what I can to take care of you.
Being there for you
No one should hurt you
I will protect you
Your indomitable power to create and do good

96
The gift of being with myself
Letting reality just be
Without my struggle
Just letting go
Letting go of my efforts
Over what I can't control
The reality

97

Personal freedom
Fully accept myself
Both shortcomings and strengths
Both fear and desire
Speaking to my inner critic and not just listening
Just being with myself

98
Everything is allowed to calm down at its own pace
Slowly sinking to the bottom
Until the water clears again
Somatic consciousness
The position of the body in the present
One step at a time and be happy with it

99

Reverence for my own wonder
That I am a creature of light
That I am a treasure
The peace flag
Because I don't have to fight anymore
To please others
To be someone else
Someone better than I am
Letting go of that struggle
Instead
Acceptance
Rest in myself
My longing is important
I am important

100

It pains me to see you suffer

But you are highly sensitive and have been hurt and scarred
by life

By trying to live a lifestyle that does not suit you

Like being out in the sun and burning your skin earlier than
others

Because your skin is so

More sensitive than the others

That is your reality

You can still sunbathe

But in your own way

You can still live your life

But in your own way

Not in the others' way

Despite your

Damages

Scars

Limitations

Are you still you

I would like to wish you more space

That you can accept yourself

For who you are

Letting go of efforts

The struggle

You don't have to live like others

Because you are not like others

Create a context that suits you

101

Hey you

My beloved inner child

You are so full of life, desire, curiosity and goodness

There is something I want to tell you

Ask you to

I am so sorry for the way I have treated you

So, I'm sorry

Because I

Criticized you

Reduced you

Made you think there is something wrong with you

You can be exactly as you are

Feel all your emotions

Wherever you are

No matter how you feel

I want to be there for you

Unconstrained

Without pressure

Just acceptance with gentle eyes and friendly voice

I ask for forgiveness

Eric Rosenqvist runs his own business as an environmental consultant and independent author. Eric writes both non-fiction and fiction for both children and adults. Eric's stories move between different topics and genres.

You can find many of Eric's stories here>>> Amazon.com : eric rosenqvist

Eric rosenqvist - Böcker | Bokus bokhandel

https://ericrosenqvist.com/